Dedication

This book is dedicated to the **Holy Spirit**, who inspired me to complete it in a week.

Acknowledgements

To my brother Ken and sister Margaret.

The heralds of purity: Jenaifa, Amanda, Buena, Maggie, Kezia, Fosuhemaa, Huda, Christie and Doris, who played a role in the realization of this dream. You are faithful stewards who have embraced the vision of the ministry and are running hard with it.

Special thanks to Mr. Kwasi Asante Opoku, my brother in Christ who helped review every single chapter. Your corrections helped reach our goal of simplicity.

To Mrs. Kabby Owusu my mentor and big sister in Christ. Thank you for giving ear to my many calls and inspiring me to keep going.

To Ps. Roderick Agyekum, my pastor, my friend and my leader. Thank you for being a good example to follow.

Finally, to my wonderful husband Paapa Mensah-Kane who gave me the peace of mind, spiritual and emotional support that I needed to write this book.

Foreword

I have been actively involved in youth ministry for well over twenty years.

From the first day the Holy Spirit impressed on my heart my calling to youth ministry, He gave me the desire to help young people in the area of their sexuality; what it entails, the challenges involved and the actual purpose God has for them regarding sex.

It is no topic for debate the confusion the subject of sex causes in the myriad of youth. The misconceptions, myths, and truths pertaining to sex have all been amassed and released into the public domain. Unfortunately, this influences young people greatly, and they are left as orphans to figure out the false from the genuine.

Sex is good because God created sex, and everything God creates is good. However, over the ages, it has been manipulated and disfigured by an evil teacher; the devil. He has led a campaign to misconstrue truths about sex and misinform the world. In sharp contrast, God has bestowed upon us the ability to seek and find the truth of His creation.

I am beside myself with joy that the sole purpose of this book is to promote the mind of God concerning sex. I am convinced, without a shadow of doubt, that this book is by all standards a true representation of God's desire concerning the management of our sexuality.

Pastor Roderick Agyekum

Founder & President,
Christ For Youth International

Introduction

After accepting Jesus Christ and making Him Lord over lives, we wish that our lives would be automatically free of sin without any input from us. Well, as nice as that sounds, it doesn't often happen. Jesus Christ saves our soul and spirit, but we have to train our body and mind to be obedient to His word.

Many Christians struggle with sexual immorality. Some don't even attempt to live a life of sexual purity. Those who care about their reputation decide to live two different lives; in public they appear pious but in private, their lives are full of immorality. Others want to please God but do not know where to start. As Christians, God desires that we live in purity whether in public or in private.

This handbook is a simple and easy guide to sexual purity. The words are straightforward and the questions in the study sessions will serve as a guide as you apply the principles to real life situations. It is designed for small group discussions, as well as personal quiet time study.

It is my earnest prayer that this book will bless you and strengthen you as you build a relationship with Jesus Christ.

Amen!

The Sexual Purity Handbook

I am excited that you have chosen this path sexual purity through the Ministry of SetApartGirl Ghana - where we redeem you through the gospel of Jesus Christ and empower you to live in sexual purity, to the glory of His Holy name.

SetApartGirl Ghana started in 2014, but officially launched on July 23, 2016. Our focus is to educate, strengthen and encourage youth to pursue sexual purity, wherever they find themselves.

This handbook is a tool to disciple you to truly understand God's vision of sanctification for you. It has five (5) chapters which are short and easy to understand.

Using this handbook

Each chapter has 4 main sections. Use the icon for each section to find your way through the chapters.

Scripture: Take a dive into the word of God and read the Father's love letter to you, straight from the bible.

Commentary: Pause and listen to what God is telling you in the context of our discussion.

Application: This shows you what to do with the knowledge of God's word and how it should reflect in your life.

Study Sessions: Open-up and discuss what God is teaching you in a loving and supportive environment.

Table of Contents

Dedication	1
Acknowledgements	2
Foreword	3
Introduction	4
The Sexual Purity Handbook	5
The Sexual Purity Agenda	8
Journey to Restoration	10
Why Sexual Purity	14
Total Purity is Possible	18
Steps to Sexual Purity	22
Spread the Vision	30
Glossary: Verses to Memorize	33

The Sexual Purity Agenda

Does being a sexually inactive automatically make us pure? The scriptures admonish us to present our bodies as a living sacrifice. (Romans 12: 1-2) It is something to be done on purpose.

Sexual purity is more that taking a decision to stay away from having sex. It has to do with keeping your mind and body free from sexual thoughts and acts that ignite sexual feelings, with the purpose of bringing glory to God.

Some of us may have begun this journey when we were much older and had already experienced most of our firsts. 2 Corinthians 5:17 says that anyone who is in Christ is a new creation. All things are new. This includes the state of our purity.

When we accept Christ, even though we may have had sex before, God sees us through a new lens and in His eyes we are pure. Physically, our bodies might not change back to the state it was in before we had sex but spiritually, we become pure.

Virginity Versus Purity?

Virginity is only a part of the full package of purity. This means that even if we have had sex before, with a renewed mind and decision to offer our bodies as a living sacrifice to God, we are as pure as virgins.

Keeping ourselves pure becomes purposeful and pleases God when we offer our bodies as living sacrifices unto Him. No matter how colourful our past lives may have been, we can serve God with the rest of it. It is all about purpose. You can still be pure.

Purposeful Purity

Without accepting Jesus Christ as Lord and personal Saviour, it is impossible to please God. In John 14:6, Jesus says 'I am the way, the truth and the life; no one goes to the Father except through me'. Accepting Jesus Christ as Lord is the first step to living a life of sexual purity.

The sexual purity agenda is not possible without salvation. It starts by realizing your need for a saviour, because as the bible says in Romans 3:23, we are sinful beings and need a saviour to redeem us from the penalty of sin - death (Romans 6:23). Once you acknowledge that, you need to realize that Jesus Christ is the only one who can save you.

God has already made arrangements for you to be redeemed, through Christ's death on the cross. To accept His redemption, you need to confess your sinful nature and ask Him to redeem you. This can be done by saying the simple prayer below and truly meaning it.

> *'Dear Lord Jesus,*
>
> *Thank you for dying on the cross for my sin. Please forgive me. Come into my life. I receive You as my Lord and Saviour. Now, help me to live for you the rest of this life. In the name of Jesus, I pray.*
>
> *Amen.'*

Congratulations! You have now escaped the gates of hell and made it into kingdom of Heaven. After becoming born again, many things will try to steal your attention and weaken you. That is why it is important to be vigilant and sober minded. The enemy is always trying to get us to fall into sin so that he devours us. One of his tools is sexual sins.

Chapter 1: Journey to Restoration

Scripture: Luke 15:11 - 24

11 Jesus continued: "There was a man who had two sons. 12 The younger one said to his father, 'Father, give me my share of the estate.' So, he divided his property between them.

13 "Not long after that, the younger son got together all he had, set off for a distant country and there squandered his wealth in wild living.

14 After he had spent everything, there was a severe famine in that whole country, and he began to be in need. 15 So he went and hired himself out to a citizen of that country, who sent him to his fields to feed pigs.

16 He longed to fill his stomach with the pods that the pigs were eating, but no one gave him anything. 17 "When he came to his senses, he said, 'How many of my father's hired servants have food to spare, and here I am starving to death!

18 I will set out and go back to my father and say to him: Father, I have sinned against heaven and against you. 19 I am no longer worthy to be called your son; make me like one of your hired servants.'

20 So he got up and went to his father. "But while he was still a long way off, his father saw him and was filled with compassion for him; he ran to his son, threw his arms around him and kissed him. 21 "The son said to him, 'Father, I have sinned against heaven and against you. I am no longer worthy to be called your son.

'22 "But the father said to his servants, 'Quick! Bring the best robe and put it on him. Put a ring on his finger and sandals on his feet.

23 Bring the fattened calf and kill it. Let's have a feast and celebrate. 24 For this son of mine was dead and is alive again; he was lost and is found.' So, they began to celebrate. - **Luke 15:11 - 24** (NIV)

Commentary

The prodigal son made his first serious mistake when he forced his father to give him his portion of the inheritance.

His second mistake was devaluing his inheritance and squandering it on things that do not satisfy. Regardless of these mistakes, he got it right when he assessed himself, and decided to go back to his father.

Application

When we make life-changing mistakes and realize that we have gone astray, let us assess ourselves honestly and avoid running away from people who tell us the truth.

The prodigal son came to his senses and decided to change the course of his life. He was ready to humble himself before his father and take the lowest position available; anything to get to close the father again! He assessed himself and admitted that he had indeed wronged his father and deserved the father's wrath and punishment.

When we sin, let us not pretend to have forgotten. Let us humble ourselves like the prodigal son and return to the Father. When we are confronted with our mistakes and weaknesses, our initial response should be to show humility and not offence.

Let us be ready to do anything to restore our relationship with Him again. This is the journey to restoration. The place where we value the Father's mercy and forgiveness and appreciate the death and resurrection of Christ most.

On the journey to restoration, we must overcome pride, offense, shame, lack and ignorance. All these lead us to rock bottom where we cry out to God for help. The only way to be fully restored is when we humble ourselves and go back to the Father.

Welcome to that humble place, dear 'Seesta'!

Study Sessions

1. What do you think could be some petty sins the prodigal son ignored which led to his demanding his part of his inheritance?
   _____
   _____
   _____

2. What fruit of the spirit was the prodigal son lacking when he demanded his inheritance? List as many as you notice. (Refer to Galatians 5:22-23 for the fruit of the spirit)
   _____
   _____
   _____

3. When the prodigal son came to his senses, what fruit of the spirit did he exhibit? According to Galatians 5:22-23 (List as many as you can count)
   _____
   _____
   _____

4. Do you see yourself in the story of the prodigal son? In what way?
   _____
   _____
   _____

5. According to this study, what are we to do when we make life-changing mistakes?
   _____
   _____
   _____

Chapter 2: Why Sexual Purity?

 **Scripture: Matthew 12:43-45**

When an impure spirit comes out of a person, it goes through arid places seeking rest and does not find it. Then it says, 'I will return to the house I left.' When it arrives, it finds the house unoccupied, swept clean and put in order. Then it goes and takes with it seven other spirits more wicked than itself, and they go in and live there. And the final condition of that person is worse than the first. That is how it will be with this wicked generation. - Matthew 12:43-45

Commentary

After the possessed man was delivered from impure spirits, he did three things. He remained unoccupied, clean and in order.

To be unoccupied can be interpreted to mean, he did not get involved with godly activities that will help spiritual growth. Godly activities like praying, fellowshipping, bible study and telling others about his deliverer Jesus Christ.

The 'clean' from the verse can be interpreted to mean he was safe and afraid to go deeper. He was clean from persecutions, from criticism from the world, and from rejection from old friends. He was clean because he played it safe. He was in order. He had a form of godliness but no real power. He knew how to say all the right things to pass the 'religion test'.

Demons use impure thoughts to lure us to sin. They also give idle people work to do for Satan. Lastly, they give us a worldly standard of goodness that prevents us from pursuing God's standard.

To overcome impure thoughts, let us fill our minds with God's truth from the bible. To overcome idleness, let us work for God faithfully. And to overcome the world's standard of goodness, let us set God's word as our yardstick - the very source of our identity.

Application

Impure is the opposite of pure. If an impure spirit is the devil's tool against Christians, then purity is God's tool for Christians.

Sexual immorality discredits us and makes our influence over the world numb. Sexual purity separates us from the world and solidifies our testimony as Christians.

Let us occupy ourselves with things Jesus did while on earth. He prayed, so let us pray too. He told others about God so let us tell others about God too. He often frequented the synagogues so let us also love attending church services.

Let us surrender totally to God, and not be afraid to take a bold stand for Jesus with our lifestyle and speech. When we surrender to Jesus, sexual passions will no longer rule over us.

Study Sessions

1. Can you list five sins that fall under sexual immorality?

   i) _____

   ii) _____

   iii) _____

   iv) _____

   v) _____

2. In what state did the impure spirit find the man when it returned?

   _____
   _____
   _____
   _____

3. Why is sexual purity an important tool for Christians?

   _____
   _____
   _____
   _____

4. What should we replace thoughts from the devil with?

   _____
   _____
   _____
   _____

5. What should we replace idleness with?

   _____
   _____
   _____
   _____

6. What should we replace the world's standard of goodness with?

   _____
   _____
   _____
   _____

Chapter 3: Total Purity is Possible

Scripture - Ephesians 6:13-17

13 Therefore put on the full armor of God, so that when the day of evil comes, you may be able to stand your ground, and after you have done everything, to stand. 14 Stand firm then, with the belt of truth buckled around your waist, with the breastplate of righteousness in place,

15 and with your feet fitted with the readiness that comes from the gospel of peace. 16 In addition to all this, take up the shield of faith, with which you can extinguish all the flaming arrows of the evil one. 17 Take the helmet of salvation and the sword of the Spirit, which is the word of God. - Ephesians 6:13-17

Commentary

The devil does not care about how religious we are or sound, he is after our heart. He wants us to live for him too.

With the armour of God, we will able to stand against every evil plot the devil forms against us. Put on the whole armour of God and total purity will be possible. This is what it means to stand.

- ♥ When we are lost, the helmet of salvation saves us and lays out our final destination, which is eternal life in Heaven.

- ♥ When we are confused, the belt of truth gives us clarity. Lies bring confusion, truth brings clarity and direction.

- ♥ When we are tempted to sin, the breastplate of righteousness guards our hearts.

- ♥ When our feet lead us to dark places, the readiness to proclaim the gospel of peace gives our feet direction to go to the right places to spread the gospel.

- ♥ When faced with battles, the word of God becomes the sword with which we fight.

- ♥ When in doubt, the shield of faith turns the evil arrows of doubt away from us.

Application

A life of total purity is a life that is completely focused on pleasing God. We can be totally pure. Not perfect but pure. From time to time, the evil one will attempt to wrestle us and shake our faith and the armour of God will help us stand firm. It could come in any form; a message from an ex to draw you back into past sins, bad friends whom you have left behind inviting you to hang out with them (Psalm 1:1), impure thoughts filling your mind and leading you back into sin (2 Corinthians 10:5b).

Our ultimate aim as Christians should be to please God. This means that our phone messages should please God. Our favourite form of entertainment should please God. Our jokes should please God. Our hobbies should please God. You get the picture...

When living a life of total purity, we must ask the Holy Spirit for help every time we see ourselves coming short and always have the full armour of God on. Since we are not perfect, this means every single day if not every minute.

Let us not be shy to ask God for help every time we need it. Asking God for help every time we need it trains our heart to start naturally depending on God for answers. That is a good place to be.

Study Sessions

1. List out the whole armour of God according to Ephesians 6: 13- 17.

   _____
   _____
   _____

2. When in doubt, which armour should we use?

   _____
   _____
   _____

3. Ama is confused about her gender; she thinks she is a boy in a girl's body. Ama is saved and has been baptised. What armour of God can help her gain clarity? (Discuss)

   _____
   _____
   _____
   _____
   _____
   _____

4. Fill in the blank spaces.
   i) Belt of _____

   ii) Breastplate of _____

   iii) Shield of _____

   iv) Helmet of _____

   v) Shoes of _____

   vi) The sword of _____

Chapter 4: Steps to Sexual Purity

Thumbs up!

Good job on following the discussion so far! We hope you are making use of the study sessions as well.

This chapter captures four areas that when carefully understood will make us confident about our decision to pursue sexual purity.

When we do not understand a reason for a decision, we are easily convinced to let go of it. Come on, let's take it one step at a time.

Scripture

Step 1: Abstain from Sexual Sin

For this is the will of God, your sanctification: that you should abstain from sexual immorality. - 1 Thessalonians 4:3

Step 2: Present Your Body unto God

I beseech you therefore, brethren, by the mercies of God, that ye present your bodies a living sacrifice, holy, acceptable unto God, which is your reasonable service. - Romans 12:1

Step 3: Wait Until You Are Married

Marriage is honourable in all, and the bed undefiled, but whoremongers and adulterers God will judge. - Hebrews 13:4

Step 4: Sacrifice Today for Tomorrow's Glory

When Christ who is our life appears, then you also will appear with Him in glory. - Colossians 3:4

Commentary

God's Vision for Purity: God is sovereign. Without our existence, He will still very much be God. He created us because He wanted to. He did not need our approval to create us. He called us forth to be, and we became.

To try to live outside His will is like fighting with ourselves. God does not hide His vision for us; sanctification. It is expressly stated in the bible (1 Thessalonians 4:3). We must embrace this vision.

After accepting Jesus Christ as our Lord and Saviour, the next step is to pursue this vision of God. In simple terms, abstain from all sins including sexual immorality.

Our Vision for Purity: When we do not embrace God's vision for purity, we prolong our journey and invite unnecessary distractions into our life.

As a ministry, SetApartGirl Ghana is here to hold your hands when you reach out and seek help. Our vision for purity has become a tool of revival. We, through all our programs, continue to beseech you to serve God with not only your heart, mind and soul, but also with your body.

Without our bodies, we will not be able to exist in this world. The most pleasing and acceptable way of thanking God for this body is to serve Him with it. Remember that your body is the temple of God.

Your Future Sex Life Approved by God: God does not hate sex - he created it! God values the marriage bed and wants it to be undefiled. He does not want us to be bothered by self-esteem issues and heartbreaks in our marriage.

Sex is not to be shared outside marriage. In God's perfect plan, the only person we should have sex with is our spouse. When we follow God's perfect plan for us, there will be no need for comparison or spouses not being sexually compatible with each other.

Marriage is a depiction of the union between us and Christ, and just us He demands us to be committed and spiritually intimate with Him alone; we are expected to have sex with our spouse alone.

The husband and the wife will spend their whole lifetime exploring each other's body and learning how to please each other within the process.

See? God wanted our joy to be complete, so He commanded us to abstain from fornication and adultery.

Sacrifice Today for Tomorrow's Glory: Jesus Christ knew the outcome of His death on the cross would be our salvation, so He endured the cross. He did not enjoy the cross, but He went through with it because He saw the glory ahead.

We need to be like Jesus, by withholding wrongly timed pleasure for the sake of tomorrow's glory. We can do it!

Application

God's Vision for Purity: We must embrace God's vision for purity. Some people realize they are not happy with their lifestyle of sexual immorality and pretend to be hard-core. They start making comments like "God is in my heart", "do not judge me", "I do not need to go to church to be saved" etc. These are all defence mechanisms they use when they do not want to give up their sin.

God is in our hearts and we should not judge others at all – the bible instructs us not to. Also, going to church does not mean we are saved. However, these truths do not cancel out God's vision for purity. We must live lives that agree with God's vision for purity. We must make a bold decision to leave the friends who influence us negatively behind.

We must stop alcoholism and listening to profane music and watching sexualized movies or TV series. - anything to help us live out God's vision for purity.

Our Vision for Purity: Sexual purity is not only possible for virgins but also for people with a sexually immoral past. We do not have to give up on ourselves when we make a mistake or willingly sin.

There are good things we want to do but our bodies do not do. And there are bad things we do not want to do that our bodies do. Apostle Paul explains this beautifully in Romans 7: 15-20. So, you see, you are not alone.

We must first win the battle in our minds before it manifests in our actions. We must cast all imaginations and thoughts that do not exalt the knowledge of Christ. This means if you are on the phone and the conversation is leading up to flirtations and naughtiness, stop yourself and do whatever is necessary to end the conversation.

When someone you could potentially be tempted to have sex with invites you to visit, request to meet in a public place. Before you even decide to meet, ask yourself if the meeting is necessary. Do everything possible to honour God and watch Him reward your actions.

Your Future Sex Life Approved by God: There is a promise of good satisfying, guilty free sex in our future. Sex that you will not need to lie to parents to have. Sex borne out of appreciation and not desperation. Sex that will yield results that we will like the whole world to know.

We are God's children; therefore, we should not tolerate any form of darkness. If we need to hide anything, then it is a form of darkness. If we need to lie about our relationship, then we should probably not be in it at all. If we need to hide to meet up, then we should not meet at all.

The world has embraced darkness fully, so they do all these things without finding the need to hide it. You and I are not of this world. We have accepted Jesus Christ as our saviour. We now have access to God Almighty, our Father. His standard for holiness has not changed. We cannot have a seat at both God's table and Satan's table.

When we choose God, we must honour Him with our bodies too.

Sacrifice Today for Tomorrow's Glory: Do not worry; you will have a beautiful marriage. Your age or family background does not limit God.

- ♥ Do not have sex with someone because you want him or her to marry you. Even if you have promised to marry each other. That promise is not a guarantee. Wait for the day of marriage.

- ♥ Do not have sex because you have had sex before. Our God is a God of many second chances. His plan for us is still in motion; we just have to be in right standing with Him.

- ♥ Do not have sex because you have had sex before. Our God is a God of many second chances. His plan for us is still in motion; we just have to be in right standing with Him.

- ♥ Do not have sex because you needed a favor. When we are going through a hard time, it feels like it will never end. When we do not compromise, the hard time passes, with no guilt or consequences associated with it. We feel victorious at the end of the tunnel when we do not compromise.

- ♥ Do not have sex to prove your love for anyone. Love is patient.

- ♥ Do not compromise. God will come through for you. He is never late. Do not give up.

Study Sessions

1. What five new decisions are you going to make after reading this chapter?
    i) _____

    ii) _____

    iii) _____

    iv) _____

    v) _____

2. Which scripture captures God's vision for purity for us?

   _____
   _____
   _____

3. What action should we take when we realize that we cannot do without purity?

   _____
   _____
   _____

4. Who is our original father before our earthly father?

   _____
   _____
   _____

5. Kojo Manu is your boyfriend. He wants you to have sex with him to prove how much you love him. What two reasons from this chapter can you use to say no to his request? Will you break up with him? (Discuss)

   _____
   _____
   _____
   _____
   _____
   _____

Chapter 5: Spread the Vision

Scripture - Romans 10:14

How then shall they call on him in whom they have not believed? And how shall they believe in him of whom they have not heard? And how shall they hear without a preacher? - Romans 10:14

Commentary

We must tell the world about Jesus Christ. We need to let them know what Jesus has done for us.

Until we met Jesus, we were literally as good as dead. This means that no matter the outcome of our lives, we were still headed for eternal damnation.

As soon as we encountered Jesus Christ and accepted Him as our Saviour and Lord over our lives, the outcome of our lives was determined. We were no longer bound to hell. We became citizens of heaven waiting to finally reach that glorious place.

The world has changed so much that talking about heaven and hell seems slightly awkward and uncomfortable. Nevertheless, we must not cower. That is the truth; there is heaven and there is hell. The only way out of hell is Jesus.

Let us go out and tell everyone we know this truth. And let us pray for the world, that God turns the hearts of people around the world to know and embrace this truth.

Application

Our salvation becomes more relevant and admirable when we walk in total purity.

The devil's popular strategy is to attack the credibility of Christians so that the world would doubt our testimonies. The devil does not want us to be good examples to the world. That is why he attacks the reputation of many preachers.

We must not give room to Satan. He lost this battle a long time ago. We should let him know by our actions. Submit to God, resist the devil and he will flee. (James 4:7) It works!

As we use this handbook, let us open our hearts to learn and repent from things the bible instructs us not to do.

A saved person who walks in sexual immorality is in danger of falling back. That is why we have to keep speaking on sexual purity and giving believers all the needed support to overcome sexual sin.

This is the reason for a sexual purity handbook.

Study Sessions

1. Without accepting Jesus Christ as Lord and Saviour, can we make it to heaven? (Read John 14:6, Acts 4: 11-12)

   _____
   _____
   _____
   _____

2. Why do we need to remain sexually pure as born again Christians? How does it affect our testimony as Christians?

   _____
   _____
   _____
   _____

3. What two things can we do to ensure the devil flees from us?
   i) _____
   ii) _____

Glossary

Verses to Memorize - Sexual Purity

In Psalms 119: 11 the Psalmist wrote "I have hidden your word in my heart that I might not sin against you."

Memorize the ten (10) verses below to help you pursue sexual purity. Shade the heart next to each verse when you have memorized it, and don't forget to share favorite verses.

♡ 1 Thessalonians 4:4-5 (NIV)

That each of you should learn to control your own body in a way that is holy and honorable, 5 not in passionate lust like the pagans, who do not know God.

♡ James 1:14 -15 (NIV)

But each person is tempted when they are dragged away by their own evil desire and enticed. 15 Then, after desire has conceived, it gives birth to sin; and sin, when it is full-grown, gives birth to death.

♡ 1 Corinthians 5:11 (NIV)

But now I am writing to you that you must not associate with anyone who claims to be a brother or sister but is sexually immoral or greedy, an idolater or slanderer, a drunkard or swindler. Do not even eat with such people.

♡ 1 Corinthians 6:18 (NIV)

Flee from sexual immorality. All other sins a person commits are outside the body, but whoever sins sexually, sins against their own body.

Glossary

Verses to Memorize - Renewing your mind

 Colossians 3:5 (NIV)

Put to death, therefore, whatever belongs to your earthly nature: sexual immorality, impurity, lust, evil desires, and greed, which is idolatry.

 Ephesians 5:3 (NIV)

But among you there must not be even a hint of sexual immorality, or of any kind of impurity, or of greed, because these are improper for God's holy people.

 2 Timothy 2:22 (NIV)

Flee the evil desires of youth and pursue righteousness, faith, love and peace, along with those who call on the Lord out of a pure heart.

 **1 Corinthians 6:18 (NIV)**

Flee from sexual immorality. All other sins a person commits are outside the body, but whoever sins sexually, sins against their own body.

 Psalms 119:9 (NIV)

How can a young person stay on the path of purity? By living according to your word.

 Romans 13:14 (NIV)

Rather, clothe yourselves with the Lord Jesus Christ, and do not think about how to gratify the desires of the flesh.

Glossary

Verses to Memorize - Renewing Your Mind

 Proverbs 4:23 (NIV)

Above all else, guard your heart, for everything you do flows from it.

 Romans 12:2 (NIV)

Do not conform to the pattern of this world but be transformed by the renewing of your mind. Then you will be able to test and approve what God's will is—his good, pleasing, and perfect will.

 Jude 1: 20 (NIV)

But you, dear friends, by building yourselves up in your most holy faith and praying in the Holy Spirit, ²¹ keep yourselves in God's love as you wait for the mercy of our Lord Jesus Christ to bring you to eternal life.

 Colossians 3:16 (NIV)

Let the message of Christ dwell among you richly as you teach and admonish one another with all wisdom through psalms, hymns, and songs from the Spirit, singing to God with gratitude in your hearts.

 2 Corinthians 5:17 (NIV)

Therefore, if anyone is in Christ, he is a new creation: the old is gone, the new has come.

 John 8:32 (NIV)

Then you will know the truth, and the truth will set you free.

Glossary

Verses to Memorize - Renewing Your Mind

 Colossians 3:2-3 (NIV)

2 Set your minds on things above, not on earthly things. 3 For you died, and your life is now hidden with Christ in God.

 Romans 8:6 (NIV)

The mind governed by the flesh is death, but the mind governed by the Spirit is life and peace.

 Hebrews 12:1 (NIV)

Therefore, since we are surrounded by such a great cloud of witnesses, let us throw off everything that hinders and the sin that so easily entangles. And let us run with perseverance the race marked out for us.

 Romans 12:21 (NIV)

Do not be overcome by evil but overcome evil with good.

Glossary

Verses to Memorize - Renewing Your Mind

 1 John 4:4 (NIV)

You, dear children, are from God and have overcome them, because the one who is in you is greater than the one who is in the world.

 Revelations 12:11a (NIV)

They triumphed over him by the blood of the Lamb and by the word of their testimony.

 Colossians 2:15 (NIV)

And having disarmed the powers and authorities, he made a public spectacle of them, triumphing over them by the cross.

 John 12:31 (NIV)

Now is the time for judgment on this world; now the prince of this world will be driven out.

 Romans 8:37 (NIV)

No, in all these things we are more than conquerors through him who loved us.

Personal Testimony

My name is Doris, and I testify of God's redemptive power, love and ability to change our stories when we allow HIM in.

Years ago, I looked for love in the wrong places and did many sexual things I am not proud of. I found God again in my lowest state and realized He never left.

He strengthened my mind, body and soul and I decided to submit fully to HIM, especially my love life and virginity. By HIS grace and strength, I was able to keep myself pure and to be an encouragement to my boyfriend, now husband, to remain pure for 2 years in our relationship.

I experienced so much peace and grew in my walk with HIM. I thank God that He saved me from the destruction I was getting deeper into, gave me a new beginning, a voice to tell of HIS goodness and that HE found me worthy to experience the bliss of marriage. Purity is possible with God's help.

Mrs. Doris Asiedu
P.R.O., SetApartGirl Ghana

Personal Testimony

I first heard of SetApartGirl Ghana in 2014, in my first year of university, through a friend. I followed her to a meeting just out of curiosity to see what this 'all-girl' group was about.

Well, fast-forward to six years later, I am still a member of this wonderful group. Before joining the ministry, I had extreme self-esteem issues, was addicted to reading romance novels, which often gave way to having all sort of fantasies and had an unhealthy view of relationships.

Through the unadulterated word of God taught here and my understanding of sexual purity, I can humbly say that I have surrendered all these unhealthy fantasies of love to God, trusting in His plan of a fruitful marriage for myself. I also know the value of myself in God's eyes and how much He loves me.

Over the years, there have been moments where I fell, but I got back up, knowing that God still loves me, and His grace is sufficient in my weakness.

Ms. Jennifer Gyasi
President, SetApartGirl Ghana